New Jersey

A PHOTOGRAPHIC PORTRAIT

PHOTOGRAPHY BY

William Taylor

First published in the United States
of America by:

Twin Lights Publishers, Inc.
8 Hale Street
Rockport, Massachusetts 01966
Telephone: (978) 546-7398
http://www.twinlightspub.com

ISBN: 1-885435-90-8
ISBN: 978-1-885435-90-3

10 9 8 7 6 5 4 3 2 1

George Washington Bridge *(opposite)*
Fort Lee

One of the world's busiest bridges,
the magnificent "GW" crosses the
Hudson River and connects upper
Manhattan, New York with Fort Lee,
New Jersey.

(frontispiece)
Cape May Lighthouse
Cape May

(jacket front)
Hunterdon Museum of Art
Clinton

(jacket back)
Ocean City Beach
Ocean City

Editorial researched and written by:
Francesca Yates and Duncan Yates

Book design by:
SYP Design & Production, Inc.
www.sypdesign.com

Printed in China

It has been said that New Jersey's greatest natural resource is its location. With New York City to the north, Pennsylvania to the west, Delaware to the southwest, and the Atlantic Ocean to the east, the "Garden State" is part of the sprawling metropolitan areas of New York and Philadelphia. Millions of residents cross state lines each day to go to work, creating a vast network of affluent and middle-class communities across the Hudson River from New York, and across the Delaware River from Philadelphia. New Jersey has more millionaire residents than any other state in America because so many Fortune 500 executives and business owners live here.

Originally settled by Dutch and Swedish immigrants in the early 1600s, New Jersey became a pivotal battlefield of the American Revolutionary War. After facing defeat at the hands of the British in New York and New Jersey in the early months of the war, General George Washington led his troops across the icy Delaware River in a Christmas Day surprise attack at the famous Battle of Trenton. It was the first of a series of victories that gave the colonists enough confidence to persevere. Washington's headquarters in Kingston is known as the military capital of the Revolution.

From densely populated cities of Newark and Jersey City and the neon casinos of Atlantic City, to the famous resorts on the Jersey Shore and the pristine beauty of the Delaware Water Gap, New Jersey, with its nearly nine million residents, is an ever-changing tapestry. The white, sandy beaches and action-packed boardwalks of Wildwood, Mount Pleasant, Seaside Heights, and other resort towns along the 127-mile-long Jersey Shore attract vacationers from around the world.

In this photographic portrait, William Taylor presents dynamic images of New Jersey, from the historic resorts of Cape May at the southernmost tip, to the fragile, protected beauty of the Meadowlands, just minutes from New York City's Times Square. Tour the historic sites along the Delaware-Raritan Canal State Park and the Charles Lindbergh estate on the forested ridges of the Highlands. Explore the Great Swamp National Wildlife Refuge and paddle along the river through the spectacular Delaware Water Gap. Discover the cultural and historic treasures of New Jersey, and the vast and surprising natural resources of this diverse and beautiful state.

Cranbury, New Jersey *(opposite)*

A directional sign at an intersection in the historic town of Cranbury, New Jersey illustrates the diversity of the "Garden State" with the names of densely populated cities such as Jersey City, Newark and the smaller rural towns of Princeton, Hightstown, and Penn's Neck.

View from Jersey City (*top*)

A golden sunset on New York Harbor creates silhouettes of Ellis Island and Liberty Island. Jersey City is directly across the harbor from Lower Manhattan's financial district. During the 19th and early 20th centuries, the arrival of thousands of European immigrants who crossed the Atlantic with hopes of a better life in America was documented on Ellis Island.

New York Waterway Ferry (*bottom*)

Since 1986, the multi-purpose fleet of New York Waterway has served 65 million commuters and tourists traveling between New Jersey and New York. With ten docks in New Jersey and seven in Manhattan, the ferries provide a scenic and convenient way to travel to Manhattan or to tour New York Harbor.

Manhattan Skyline (*opposite*)

Manhattan skyscrapers bask in the warm light of the setting sun. Some of the most spectacular views of New York City can be seen from the Jersey City waterfront.

The Newark Museum *(top)*

New Jersey's largest art museum, The Newark Museum, includes eighty galleries of art from sixteen countries. The museum opened in 1909 with a definitive collection of Tibetan art. One of the museum's most renowned exhibits, Picturing America, is considered one of the most exquisite collections of American art in the country.

Historic Ballantine House *(bottom)*

The Decorative Arts Wing of The Newark Museum is housed in the restored 27-room Ballantine House, former home of legendary brewer John Holme Ballantine. A National Historic Landmark, the mansion showcases the luxurious lifestyle of the Ballentines in eight rooms of Victorian-period decor. Displayed are decorative objects from the 1650s to present.

Newark Fire Museum *(opposite)*

This vintage 1857 pump-and-pull fire truck is an excellent example of firefighting apparatus used during the mid-19th century. It is part of an extensive collection of antique equipment and memorabilia exhibited in the Newark Fire Museum located on the grounds of The Newark Museum.

Cathedral Basilica of the Sacred Heart *(opposite)*

Cathedral Basilica of the Sacred Heart in Newark was constructed between 1899 and 1954. It is the fifth largest cathedral in the United States. Although originally designed in the English-Irish Gothic style, the cathedral reflects the French Gothic style in Chartres, Laon, and Rheims. It was elevated to Basilica status by Pope John Paul II in 1995.

Branch Brook Park *(above)*

Branch Brook Park is the first county park in the United States to be opened to the public. Located across the lake from Cathedral Basilica of the Sacred Heart, the park features open meadowland and woodlands on a gently rolling terrain. Graceful paths and roadways curve around the park's 2,000 cherry trees. Every spring the Cherry Blossom Festival attracts large crowds.

Liberty Science Center *(above)*

Located in beautiful Liberty State Park in Jersey City, the Liberty Science Center re-opened in 2007 with a new mission: to not only help the community learn about science, but to help people become active in science. The museum includes the new 20,000-square-foot Center for Science Learning and Teaching.

Liberty State Park *(opposite)*

Liberty State Park, located on the Hudson River waterfront in Jersey City, commands spectacular views of New York Harbor, Manhattan, the Statue of Liberty, and historic Ellis Island. Park visitors can board ferries to the Statue of Liberty, Ellis Island, and Lower Manhattan. The park opened in 1976, in honor of America's Bicentennial.

Statue of Liberty National Monument *(opposite)*

A short ferry ride from Jersey City's Liberty State Park is one of the most famous symbols of freedom in America, the Statue of Liberty. Designed by Frédéric Auguste Bartholdi, the statue was a gift from France given to the people of the United States in 1886. Ellis Island, where European immigrants first set foot in America, is also part of this national complex.

Sandy Hook *(above)*

Sandy Hook, a beautiful barrier peninsula on the Jersey Shore, is also a National Park. Seven miles of spectacular ocean and bay beaches attract surf casters, swimmers, and sunbathers. A military base is located on the peninsula as well as the country's oldest operating lighthouse. Sandy Hook is also an area frequented by over 300 species of migratory birds.

Jenkinson's Amusement Park *(opposite, top and bottom)*

Jenkinson's Amusement Park and Boardwalk, located in Point Pleasant, has been a source of family fun and entertainment for many years. The park has expanded to include a number of thrilling rides and attractions such as the newly acquired Moby Dick, and an old-fashioned fun house, with two floors of challenging obstacles, and baffling twists and turns.

Jenkinson's Lucky's *(above)*

While a parasailer and a seagull fly high above Point Pleasant, sunbathers enjoy the beach next to Jenkinson's Amusement Park and Boardwalk. When the park opened in 1927, the sleepy beach town was transformed into a popular Jersey Shore attraction. The Boardwalk features an arcade, an aquarium, and a 1,200-seat pavilion with live entertainment, restaurants, and bars.

Funtown Pier *(above and left)*

A daring young park patron bounces high above the extreme trampoline of Funtown Pier's 5 Unit Trampoline ride at Seaside Park. In the distance, the Loop Roller Coaster is an exhilarating adventure consisting of hair-raising twists and turns. The amusement pier extends out over the Atlantic Ocean on a beautiful stretch of Barnegat Peninsula, a barrier island on the Jersey Shore.

Sunbathing at Seaside Park

Soft sands of the expansive beach at Seaside Park
stretch for two miles along the Jersey Shore on
Barnegat Peninsula. During the summer months,
families enjoy the pristine beach and the beauty
of the Atlantic Ocean with all of the fishing,
swimming, and surfing it has to offer, as well
as the non-stop thrills and attractions at
Funtown Pier.

American Legion Post No. 213 *(above)*

A lone cannon rests silently on the lawn while flags wave in the breeze in front of the American Legion Post No. 213 in rural Sussex. Not far from the High Point Monument, the post was one of thousands opened in 1919 by the American Legion after World War I to aid and comfort American war veterans.

High Point Monument *(opposite)*

Built in 1930 to honor all war veterans, the obelisk-style monument rises 220 feet atop a hill in High Point, the highest peak in the Kittatinny Mountains and the highest point in New Jersey. The monument's observatory provides panoramic views of the Pocono Mountains to the west, the Catskills to the north, and the Wallkill River Valley.

Mordecai Boat Basin *(above)*

A sportfishing boat docks at a quiet Mordecai Boat Basin in Beach Haven, a town on southern New Jersey's Long Beach Island. The boat basin is sheltered by Mordecai Island, an uninhabited coastal marsh island. In the late 19th century, wealthy residents of Philadelphia transformed the town of Beach Haven into a popular beach-front resort.

Barnegat Light *(opposite)*

Although lighthouses have stood on the north end of Long Beach Island since 1835, Barnegat Light wasn't built until 1856. The second tallest in the United States, this current lighthouse operated until 1927 at which time it was replaced by Barnegat Lightship eight miles offshore. Visited by many summertime lighthouse enthusiasts, this historic light is illuminated by floodlight at night.

Historic Smithville *(opposite, above, and right)*

Fifteen miles from the glitz of Atlantic City, Historic Smithville is a charming village of cobblestone streets, riverside boardwalks, and quaint shops housed in authentic, late 18th-century buildings. During the American Revolution, privateers smuggled goods into the country along the river during the British occupation of Philadelphia. With unique shopping and old-fashioned carousel and train rides, Historic Smithville is a favorite family destination. Shops offer one-of-a-kind items such as British, Irish, and Italian imports, books, antiques, music, jewelry, teas, candles, and collectibles. A restaurant in the historic Smithville Inn, formerly a stagecoach inn, provides intimate dining.

Bally's Wild, Wild West Casino *(above and opposite)*

One of Bally's three casinos, the Wild, Wild West Casino invites guests to test their luck in an old Western mining town, complete with a painted, prairie sky forty feet above the gaming tables. The western theme begins outside on the boardwalk with a twenty-foot mountain, waterfalls, mines, and animatronic figures that talk about their frontier adventures. Inside the 74,000-square-foot casino, guests can play a variety of games of chance from slots and video poker to higher-stakes poker, blackjack, baccarat, craps, and the roulette wheel. On-site restaurants include the Gold Rush Grill & Saloon, Virginia City Buffet, and the Lone Star Snack Bar.

Schiff's Central Pier

An Atlantic City landmark, Schiff's Central Pier is one of the oldest buildings on the Boardwalk. Located along the 1920s art-deco pavilion are attractions such as carnival booth games, video games, laser tag, and a racecar speedway. An array of boardwalk shops feature souvenirs and pizza parlors.

Ripley's Believe It or Not!

In a display of architectural whimsy, a gigantic earth-shaped wrecking ball crashes through the façade of Atlantic City's Ripley's Believe It or Not! museum. True to its reputation, Ripley's offers fascinating, funny, and often creepy exhibits including a roulette wheel made of jelly beans, shrunken heads, and many other incredible phenomena.

Steel Pier (top)

The bright lights and attractions of legendary Steel Pier stretch far out over the Atlantic Ocean. Rebuilt and enhanced, the historic 1898 pier features rides, games, prize wheels, and a wide assortment of delicious foods. A unique double-decker carousel, crafted by Italian artisans, features hand-painted scenes depicting Atlantic City's past.

Steel's Fudge (bottom)

Dubbed "the best fudge on the Jersey Shore," Steel's Fudge has long lived up to its reputation. Elizabeth Steel opened her sweets shop in 1919, and nearly one-hundred years later, her grandchildren carry on the tradition. No trip to Atlantic City is complete without this delicious indulgence.

The Pier Shops at Caesars (opposite)

Emulating the style of the Forum Shops at Caesars Palace in Las Vegas, the Atlantic City resort and casino has expanded to include the luxurious Pier Shops at Caesars. The impressive $175 million addition features one-hundred shops and nine restaurants on four levels, and is conveniently accessible by a skywalk from the resort.

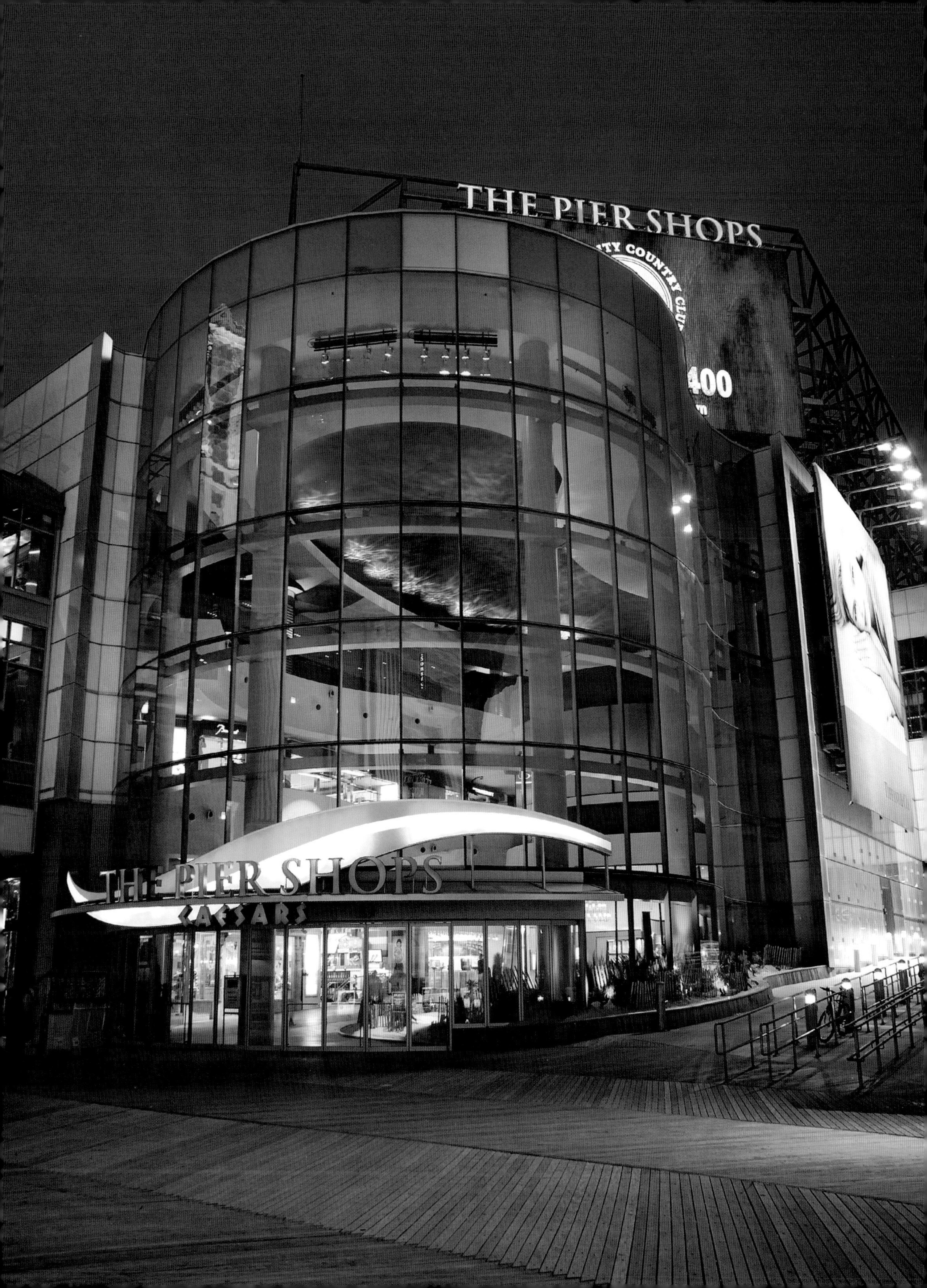
THE PIER SHOPS
THE PIER SHOPS
CAESARS

Caesars Atlantic City *(above)*

Under the cloud-covered, blue-sky ceiling mural at Caesars Palace, Roman statues encircle an opulent lobby and welcome guests to an unparalleled Atlantic City experience. The lavish days of ancient Rome are celebrated in painstaking detail from the four-story atrium to the impressive sculptures, sparkling fountains, and gleaming marble floors.

Caesars Palace *(opposite)*

An imposing statue of the first Emperor of Rome, Caesar Augustus, stands in the lobby of Caesars Atlantic City. With an area over 100,000 square feet and 3,400 slot machines, the resort's casino is one of the largest in the city. Circus Maximus, the resort's performance hall, features headliners such as Celine Dion, Bill Cosby, and Martina McBride.

CAESAR
AUGUSTUS
First Roman Emperor
63 B.C. to
14 C.E.

CAESARS

Garden Pier *(top)*

With a more sophisticated vision in mind, the Spanish Renaissance architecture and beautifully landscaped gardens of the 1913 Garden Pier set it apart from the hustle and bustle of other amusement park themed piers in Atlantic City. Garden Pier is the fitting location of the Atlantic City Art Center and the Atlantic City Historical Museum.

Atlantic City Art Center *(bottom)*

The opening of the Atlantic City Art Center in 1953 began a new era of revitalization for the Garden Pier. The art center's three exhibition galleries change monthly and showcase contemporary artists of national, regional, and local fame. In addition to art exhibits, visitors enjoy concerts, artists' demonstrations, and literary readings that the center offers.

Mr. Peanut Makes History

The familiar Planter's Mr. Peanut, a much beloved American icon, relaxes on a bench in front of the Atlantic City Historical Museum. The famous peanut is part of the colorful history of Atlantic City on display inside the museum. A six-foot version of Mr. Peanut stood in front of Planter's Peanut shop on the boardwalk from 1930 to 1978.

Sea Lessons

To understand marine life and maritime ways more fully, the Ocean Life Education Center, located in historic Gardner's Basin, provides a hands-on computerized environment. Visitors can experience the challenges of sailing using a model sailboat and a wind tunnel, feel the power of the ocean at the Ship's Bridge exhibit, and watch as divers feed stingrays and sharks.

Atlantic City Aquarium *(top and bottom)*

Groman, a giant Loggerhead Turtle, is one of over one-hundred species at the Atlantic City Aquarium, in historic Gardner's Basin. Fish of the New Jersey Coast is one of seventeen tanks showcasing giant moray eels, seahorses, jellyfish, an octopus, a coral reef, small sea creatures, and other exotic marine life.

Tun Tavern Brewery and Restaurant

Atlantic City's award-winning Tun Tavern, with its modern casual setting, carries on the long tradition of the original 17th-century Tun Tavern in Philadelphia, Pennsylvania, one of the first brew pubs in colonial America. The fine restaurant's delectably mouthwatering menu and premium selection of beers has earned it national recognition.

Lucy the Elephant, Margate

Built as an attraction when Atlantic City was a
Victorian beach resort in the 1880s, Lucy the
Elephant is a gigantic structure that continues to
appeal to passersby from near and far. Ship logs
confirm that the six-story elephant is visible on
a clear day from eight miles out at sea, making
Lucy the only elephant-shaped navigational
device in the world.

Gillian's Wonderland Pier *(opposite)*

The towering 141-foot Giant Wheel provides extraordinary sweeping views of Ocean City and, on a clear day, Atlantic City. In addition to the many rides and attractions at Gillian's Wonderland Pier, the amusement complex has grown to include wet-and-wild Gillian Island Water Park and the Adventure Golf Course for mini-golfers.

The Midway at Wonderland Pier *(above)*

The midway at Wonderland Pier is filled with fun and exciting excursions including Bear Affair, where youngsters can jump inside Wonder Bear and take a spinning ride. The Musik Express gives passengers an exhilarating rock-'n-roll ride, while the Galleon invites brave venturers to hold on tight while the gyrating motion of the ocean takes over.

41

Ocean City Beach *(top)*

Twenty minutes from Atlantic City at the northern tip of Cape May County, Ocean City is a world-renowned beachfront community that is an easy ride from New York, Pennsylvania, and all points in New Jersey. Voted one of the world's best boardwalks, its 2.5-mile stretch features Gillian's Wonderland Pier, shops, restaurants, and movie theaters.

Historic City Hall *(bottom)*

The 1914 City Hall at Ocean City is one of over two hundred vintage buildings in the Ocean City Historic District. It is a striking example of the grandeur of public buildings erected during the "City Beautiful" movement of the early 20th century. Vivian Smith, a prominent architect of southern New Jersey coastal communities, detailed the majestic building with terra cotta.

Boardwalk Playhouse

A playground on the North Ocean City boardwalk invites youngsters to stop by and have fun. Little tykes can climb aboard brightly colored bi-planes and fly around a circular track. Older kids can go to the Playhouse, "take a screen test," and see themselves on television. The Ocean City boardwalk is known for its miles of continuous amusement rides and entertainment venues.

The Wetlands Institute *(above and opposite)*

Overlooking 6,000 acres of pristine coastal wetlands, The Wetlands Institute in Stone Harbor promotes the preservation of salt-marsh ecosystems. This fragile natural resource is where many species of waterfowl can be seen from viewing stations. The institute's cedar-shake building was designed to resemble a 19th-century coast guard station.

With guided tours, back-bay boat rides, kayaking, animal shows, and guided beach and dune walks, The Wetlands Institute lives up to its slogan, "The Natural Place to Have Fun." The beauty of the wetlands inspired the Wings 'n Water Festival, one of the premier wildlife arts festivals in the country.

South Jersey Wetlands *(pages 46–47)*

The vast and beautiful wetlands of Southern New Jersey along with the native species of waterfowl, fish, and shellfish are protected from encroachment by strict state laws. The wetlands are valuable contributors to the health of the earth's ecosystems and provide plentiful open spaces for recreation.

Wildwood Boardwalk *(above and left)*

The boardwalk at Wildwood includes two miles of stores, souvenir shops, restaurants, arcades and carnival-style games, as well as other beachfront attractions. Visitors can satisfy a sweet tooth with salt-water taffy and cotton candy, or enjoy a delicious seafood dinner. The 38-block boardwalk boasts of having more rides than Disneyland.

Seaport Aquarium *(opposite)*

The open jaws of a large shark at the entrance to the Seaport Aquarium in Wildwood are a fitting invitation to the Atlantic Ocean mysteries found inside. The aquarium showcases the extensive marine life of New Jersey's coastal waters. For a unique keepsake, more adventurous visitors can have their photograph taken alongside a live snake.

Morey's Piers *(above)*

The Giant Wheel towers high over one of the largest amusement piers in the world. Morey's Piers at Wildwood Beach feature over seventy fun-filled rides and attractions including two spacious beachfront waterparks. Rides range from slower-paced kiddie rides to some of the most hair-raising roller coaster excursions on the East Coast.

Sunset Beach *(top)*

Sunset Beach on Cape May Point is aptly named for its magnificent sunsets. Off shore is the wreckage of the S.S. *Atlantus*, a World War I concrete ship. After the war ended, the ship was decommissioned. Before the concrete hull of the great ship would be used as the foundation of a new Cape May ferry dock, a violent storm ran her aground.

Sunset Beach Grill *(bottom)*

The Sunset Beach Grill is a popular eatery that specializes in sandwiches, soups, salads, and finger foods. Located on the southernmost point of Cape May, Sunset Beach Grill has an unobstructed view of the horizon. The area's unique atmospheric conditions, caused by the interaction of sea breezes across the bay, create sensational vivid skies at dusk.

The Voodoo Tree (*above*)

Legend has it that well over a decade ago, an anonymous wood carver created this compelling sculpture on a tree trunk at Cape May Point. Etched on the side opposite the eerie mask are the words, "The Voodoo Tree." Since no one has ever come forward to make its claim, the curious carved image continues to be an intriguing mystery to beachgoers.

Cape May Lighthouse (*opposite*)

Built in 1853 at the southern tip of New Jersey, the historic Cape May Lighthouse continues to be a commissioned navigational aid. The lighthouse is one of the few original seacoast tower lights on the Atlantic coast. No trip to the Jersey Shore is complete without a walk up the stairs to wonder at the panoramic views from the lighthouse balcony.

Congress Hall Hotel *(opposite)*

After humble beginnings as a boarding house, the historic 1816 Congress Hall Hotel in Cape May provides elegant lodging for discriminating vacationers to this island resort town. The hotel had been the summer White House for President Benjamin Harrison in the late 19th century. John Philip Sousa later conducted the *Congress Hall March* here.

The Abbey Bed & Breakfast *(left)*

The Abbey Bed & Breakfast is an 1869 Gothic Revival mansion, located in the historic district of Cape May. The charming B&B exquisitely creates a Victorian ambiance with period architecture and antiques, along with providing excellent service. The mansion is one block from the beach, shopping, great restaurants, and close to popular birding sites.

Victorian Architechture *(right)*

Cape May boasts an array of spectacular Victorian structures that are a step back in time to this 19th-century seaside resort. By the mid 1800s, the town's popularity began to rival Providence, Rhode Island and other well-known East Coast resorts. With just over 4,000 year-round residents, Cape May welcomes thousands of vacationers every year.

Cape May *(above)*

A wooden rowboat pays a colorful homage to the popular seaside town of Cape May. As the sun casts a fading, golden light across the sky, beachfront hotels and cottages line the shore and give patrons a front-row seat to the striking scenery of the ever-changing moods of the chilly Atlantic waters.

Dramatic Sunrise *(opposite)*

A dramatic sunrise sets the skies aglow in a magnificent display on the ocean side of Cape May Island, the southernmost point of the state of New Jersey. The beachfront is impeccably clean and wide with beautiful breakers and a gentle slope. The bay side of the island includes a wildlife refuge and is the summer home for hundreds of dolphins.

Historic Batsto Village *(left, above, and opposite)*

Batsto Village is an open-air museum in the South Central Pinelands of New Jersey. From the mid-18th century to the mid-19th century, Batsto was a thriving industrial center for bog iron production and glassmaking. Listed on the National Register of Historic Places, Batsto Village features thirty-three historic buildings including a mansion, a post office, a sawmill, a gristmill, a general store, and several period houses.

Batsto Mansion

The former home to generations of ironmasters, the 32-room Batsto Mansion is located in the heart of Batsto Village, an open-air museum in the Wharton National Forest. Renovated in the elegant style of Italianate architecture, visitors can stroll through fourteen rooms, including the parlor, a dining room, a library, and several period bedrooms.

Historic Gristmill

When it was built in 1828, the Gristmill was powered by a wooden water wheel. By 1882, the wheel had become outdated and was replaced with a modern side-winder water turbine that increased the mill's efficiency. Grains such as wheat, corn, and others were processed and stored here until they were sold at the Batsto Village general store.

Cowtown Rodeo *(top)*

An enormous red bull greets motorists along Route 40 at Cowtown Rodeo near Woodstown. Each week, farmers, ranchers, and city slickers from nearby Philadelphia and Wilmington, Delaware watch the wild-west excitement of steer wrestling, bareback riding, calf roping, saddle bronc riding, bull riding, and barrel racing events.

Ride'em Cowboy *(bottom)*

Cowboys participate in a team roping competition at Cowtown Rodeo near Woodstown. The brainchild of local resident Howard "Stoney" Harris, the rodeo increased attendance at the 1929 county fair. It is now the longest running Saturday night rodeo in the United States. Stoney Harris' grandchildren now carry on the family tradition.

Roadside Cowboy *(opposite)*

With his red bull companion *(top)*, a colossal cowboy stands in front of Cowtown Rodeo and welcomes Route 40 motorists to southwestern New Jersey. The rural community of Woodstown, with miles of fertile farmland, is a sharp contrast to the densely populated cities of northern New Jersey located directly across from New York City.

Richman's Ice Cream Company

Woodstown has been satisfying its dessert crav-
ings at Richman's Ice Cream Company since
1894 when William Richman first opened the
shop. It remained in the family until the 1980s
and was then sold to another family who continues the delicious tradition today. Richman's is a
favorite stop for tourists who are in Woodstown
for the rodeo or flea market and auction.

Haystacks

Bales of hay are neatly stacked under a protective shelter on a farm in Woodstown, a town with a population of approximately 3,000 residents. This rural area is located only thirteen miles from Wilmington, Delaware and twenty-two miles from Philadelphia. Over ninety percent of Woodstown residents commute to work across state lines.

Barclay Homestead
(above, left, and opposite)

Now a living heritage museum, the historic Barclay Homestead, located in Cherry Hill, is an 1816 federal-style brick farmhouse built by Quaker Joseph Thorn. It provides year-round public tours, programs and events to teach visitors about 19th-century Quaker farm life. Local gardeners participate in the museum's Plant a Patch program where they grow their own fruits and vegetables on 25-foot square plots.

Battleship U.S.S. New Jersey *(top)*

The most decorated battleship in American history is now a floating museum on the Camden waterfront across from Center City, Philadelphia. The Battleship U.S.S. *New Jersey* was commissioned in 1943 for service in World War II and has served in Korea and Vietnam. She was recommissioned in 1982 in President Reagan's 600-ship Navy.

Battleship Propeller *(bottom)*

A massive propeller from the Iowa-class battleship is exhibited on the grounds of the Battleship New Jersey Museum and Memorial in Camden. In the distance, the acclaimed ship with its giant guns, awaits visitors with stories of wartime glory. The museum provides tours, events, and overnight encampments.

U.S.S. New Jersey's Big Guns *(opposite)*

Built to "keep floating and keep fighting," the U.S.S. *New Jersey* has a battery of nine 16-inch guns that have reached land targets nearly twenty-three miles away. As Admiral Halsey's flagship of the Pacific Fleet in World War II, she saw action against Japanese forces. The formidable battleship is eleven stories high and nearly three football fields long.

Benjamin Franklin Bridge *(above)*

Considered to be Philadelphia's greatest bridge, the Benjamin Franklin Bridge spans the Delaware River between Philadelphia and Camden. When it opened in 1926, it was the largest suspension bridge in the world. Today, it is one of four bridges connecting Philadelphia with southern New Jersey.

New Jersey Adventure Aquarium *(opposite)*

A well-stocked shark tank is part of the many exhibits at the New Jersey Adventure Aquarium in Camden. Penguin Island has a 20-foot underwater viewing area, while the West African river experience features hippos, free-flying birds, and porcupines. The Creature Lab has electric eels, mudskippers, flashlight fish, as well as a number of other unusual species.

The Walt Whitman Arts Center *(top)*

Housed in a historic 1918 Neo-Classical building, the Walt Whitman Arts Center focuses on
world-class artists and programs, enhancing the
cultural revitalization of Camden. In addition
to paintings, illustrations, fabric works, and
artifacts, the center provides main stage theatre
productions, music and dance programs, and
arts education outreach programs.

Camden Children's Garden *(opposite)*

Adjacent to the New Jersey Aquarium is an interactive garden for children created by the Camden
City Garden Club. The Camden Children's
Garden exhibits include a butterfly house and a
tropical exhibit. Also included are beautiful fairy-
tale themed gardens such as Alice in Wonderland
and the Frog Prince Grotto, as well as carousel
and train rides.

Historic Whitesbog Village *(above and opposite)*

The site of New Jersey's largest cranberry and blueberry farm, the village of Whitesbog is nestled in the renowned Pinelands National Reserve. The original turn-of-the-century company town remains mostly in tact with a general store, post office, school house, residences, and berry processing buildings. The cranberry is the state fruit of New Jersey.

State Legislative Chambers *(above)*

The legislative chambers of the New Jersey State House, located in Trenton, illustrate the beauty of this historic building. Although many structural changes and additions have been made, the Governor's private chambers remain in an original section of the 1792 building, making it the country's second oldest state house in continuous use.

Capitol Dome *(left)*

Restored in 1999, the magnificent gold-leaf dome rises 145 feet above the first floor. Built in 1889, it replaced an 80-foot dome that was destroyed by fire. Its design is French Academic Classical with Roman motifs. An inscription on the dome's decorative cove states, "There must be Justice even though the Heavens Fall."

New Jersey State Capitol *(opposite)*

The impressive 1792 State House reflects the popular architectural styles of the 19th and 20th centuries including Victorian and American Renaissance. Famous artworks are displayed throughout the building, while a special exhibit of artifacts and memorabilia celebrate its unique heritage.

Meredith Havens Firemen's Museum

Designed by Robert Venturi, Meredith Havens Firemen's Museum is located at the Trenton Fire Headquarters. Originally founded in 1959, the museum preserves the history of firefighting with a sharp emphasis on Trenton's unique story. The impressive collection includes antique firefighting apparatus, paraphernalia, and memorabilia.

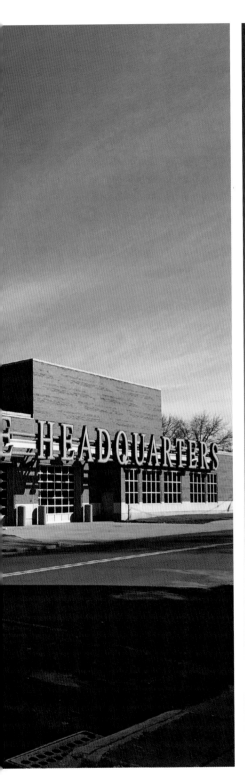

Trenton Battle Monument

High atop the 148-foot granite monument, General George Washington boldly points toward the site of the Battle of Trenton, while two Continental soldiers flank the entrance below. The 1776 battle was an important American victory and morale booster for the General's troops during the early months of the Revolutionary War.

Old Barracks Museum *(opposite)*

Both a state and national landmark, the Old
Barracks Museum housed three-hundred Irish
and English soldiers during the French and
Indian War in 1758. During the Revolutionary
War, British and Hessian troops stayed in the
barracks until they were defeated by General
George Washington's troops at the decisive Battle
of Trenton.

New Jersey State Museum *(above)*

Exhibitions at this Trenton museum represent four
collection areas. Archaeology and Ethnology covers
two million prehistoric and historic specimens.
Cultural History documents the people of New
Jersey from the 17th century to the present. The
Fine Arts collection features over 10,000 works
of art with a New Jersey focus. The Natural History
artifacts represent the oldest and most extensive
collection.

81

Grounds for Sculpture *(top and bottom)*

Detailed sculptures of a woman and child *(top)* and a scene entitled *Were You Invited?*, inspired by French Impressionist Pierre-Auguste Renoir's *Luncheon of the Boating Party (bottom)* are examples of the treasures found at Grounds for Sculpture, an acclaimed art center in Hamilton. Artistic styles range from life-like figures to bold, geometric abstracts.

Rat's Restaurant *(opposite)*

Located at Grounds for Sculpture, Rat's is a fine dining restaurant set in an elegant country chateau. The unusual name is originated from Ratty, the quintessential host in the children's book, *The Wind in the Willows*. The eclectic cuisine is paired with breathtaking views of the lush landscaping and outdoor sculptures of an internationally renowned arts center.

Sayen Park Botanical Garden
(above, right, and opposite)

This exquisite Sayen Park Botanical Garden in Hamilton, decorates thirty acres with over 1,000 azaleas, nearly 500 rhododendrons, 250,000 flowering bulbs, tranquil ponds, scenic walking trails, and graceful gazebos and bridges. A favorite place for outdoor weddings and professional portraits, the gardens opened in 1912 on the estate of Frederick Sayen and Anne Mellon Sayen, daughter of the prominent Mellon family.

Grovers Mill Company *(opposite and top)*

In 1938 Grover's Mill was identified as the Martian invasion landing site on Orson Wells' infamous radio broadcast, *War of the Worlds*. The broadcast sounded so realistic that it launched a mass panic across the United States. It has been said that the writer of the radio show discovered the name, *Grover's Mill*, by throwing a dart at a map of New Jersey.

Grover's Mill is an unincorporated area located in West Windsor Township near Trenton and Princeton University. Joseph H. Grover bought the existing mill in 1868. He eventually opened a flour and feed store in Princeton. Over time, the Grover family owned all the properties in the area.

Stults Farm *(above)*

From strawberries and peas in summer to pumpkins and Indian corn in autumn, Stults Farm in the small town of Cranbury is busy growing a wide variety of fruits and vegetables. Fresh produce lovers can pick their own or shop at the farm's roadside stand. One of many privately owned New Jersey farms, Stults dates back to 1915.

George Washington's Headquarters *(opposite)*

Rockingham State Historic Site is an 18th-century structure that served as the temporary headquarters of General George Washington during the final months of the Revolutionary War in 1783. It was here that Washington received the news that the Treaty of Paris had been signed and America had won its freedom from England.

Delaware & Raritan Canal *(opposite)*

Low limbs bow gracefully over the Delaware & Raritan Canal, a choice waterway for canoeing and catch-and-release fishing. Part of the canal runs parallel to the Delaware River and passes by the historic village of Griggstown in Franklin Township. A biking and walking trail follows an old rail line alongside the scenic canal.

Delaware & Raritan Canal State Park *(above)*

The 19th-century Bridgetender's House and Station is one of several remaining structures in the historic district of Griggstown, located on the banks of the Delaware & Raritan Canal. The canal was originally built across the middle of New Jersey to transport freight between New York and Philadelphia. Over sixty miles of the canal are now a state park.

Carnegie Lake *(opposite)*

A Princeton University rowing team glides across Carnegie Lake near the Washington Street Bridge on the south end of campus. Over three miles long, the lake was the brainchild of Princeton graduate Howard Russell Butler and steel tycoon Andrew Carnegie at the turn of the 20th century. It is home to Princeton's crew program and training site for many past Olympic rowing teams.

Princeton University Chapel *(top)*

A campus landmark, the 1927 Princeton University Chapel is a splendid example of collegiate Gothic-style architecture. The builiding is constructed from Pennsylvania sandstone and Indiana limestone, and has a capacity of 2,000. The chapel's magnificent stained glass windows depict not only religious scenes, but scenes of Science, Law, Poetry, and War as well.

Historic Drumthwacket Mansion

The official residence of the governor of New Jersey, Drumthwacket is listed on the National Register of Historic Places. Steeped in history, the 1830s mansion was built for wealthy business-man Charles Smith Olden. Olden became a trustee for the College of New Jersey, now Princeton University, and was the first governor to live at Drumthwacket.

Drumthwacket Grounds

Drumthwacket, which means *wooded hill* in Scottish Gaelic, is situated near the site of the American victory at the 1777 Battle of Trenton. The mansion's grounds are elegantly landscaped with formal Italianate gardens, broad walkways, bridal paths, and sculptures. The mansion and grounds are open for tours.

Princeton Monthly Meeting
of the
Religious Society of Friends
Meeting for Worship
Each First Day 9 & 11

First Day School
11:00 October thru May

Princeton
Friends School

Quaker Meeting House *(opposite)*

The first Europeans to settle in the Princeton area during the 1690s were six Quaker families. They built their first Meeting House in 1726 and their current one in 1760. A New Jersey dignitary who signed the Declaration of Independence is buried in the adjacent graveyard. The Meeting House is on the National Register of Historic Sites.

Washington Crossing State Park *(above)*

Washington Crossing State Park honors the site where General George Washington and his troops crossed the Delaware River and won the Revolutionary War Battle of Trenton. The bucolic park is also known for the beauty of its nature trails, wildlife habitat, and forests of Japanese larch, Norway spruce, and Eastern white and red pines.

Historic Johnson Ferry House *(top)*

The circa 1740 farmhouse and nearby tavern were owned by Garret Johnson, the man who also ran the ferry service across the Delaware River. The house was used briefly by General Washington and other officers during the famous crossing from Pennsylvania. The rooms are furnished with antiques similar to those used in the 18th century.

Site of Crossing *(bottom)*

A simple stone wall marks the area where General George Washington and his troops crossed the Delaware River in the cold, pre-dawn hours of Christmas Day, 1776 to win the pivitol Battle of Trenton. The successful sneak attack on the British yielded the capture of thirty officers and over 1,000 soldiers without one single American fatality.

Delaware and Raritan Canal *(opposite)*

Eighteenth-century stone and clapboard structures dot the shoreline between the canal and the Delaware River in this historic state park. A section of the forty-four-mile canal flows through the 3,000-acre park. Built fifty years after the Revolutionary War, the canal provides water for much of central New Jersey.

Howell Living History Farm

The Howell Living History Farm in New Jersey's Pleasant Valley Historic District is a unique educational venue that lets visitors experience what farming was like during the dawn of the 20th century. Depending on the time of year, guests of this working farm can help plant, cultivate, and harvest crops; care for the animals; or make soap, butter, and ice cream.

100

Visiting the Past

History is recreated every day on 45 acres at Howell Living History Farm in Lambertville. The staff authentically recreates a typical mixed crop and livestock family farm at the turn-of-the-century. The farm animals are descendants of breeds raised in the valley in 1900. Visitors can observe restoration work in progress at the main barn and farmhouse.

Golden Nugget Antique Market *(above and opposite)*

The Golden Nugget Antique Market has attracted the most savvy antique hunters and bargain browsers since 1967. The East Coast's premier market for vintage and retro items, shoppers come here to find that special antique or collectible. Many of the Golden Nugget's loyal antique dealers have showcased their wares here for twenty or thirty years.

The name "Golden Nugget" celebrates legendary Lambertville native, James W. Marshall, the man who first discovered gold and started the great California Gold Rush in 1848. Regular antique market shoppers often feel like they've struck gold when they find the perfect antique for their home or a rare item for their collections.

The sheer volume of merchandise available at the Golden Nugget includes everything from books, dolls, and clocks to china, garden items, and hardware. Inside, many dealers have separate rooms that showcase vintage furniture, art, jewelry, Victorian collectibles, coins, stamps, model trains, and much more.

OPEN
MORE DEALERS INSIDE

INSIDE DEALER SPACE AVAILABLE
PAY LESS THAN SELF STORAGE !
INQUIRE AT OFFICE OR CALL:
609 - 397 - 0811

St. John the Evangelist Parish *(opposite and above)*

In 1842, the original building for St. John the Evangelist Parish was erected in Lambertville, giving it the distinction of being the first Catholic church in Hunterdon County. The current Gothic Revival-style church was built in 1896 just a few blocks from the original site. In spring, blossoming gardens create their own kind of sanctuary.

Mount Zion Methodist Episcopal Church

The Mount Zion Methodist Episcopal Church, located in the Sourland Mountains Region of the state, was constructed in 1843, and later rebuilt in 1880. The Sourland Mountains, often referred to as New Jersey's last great wilderness, is home to many animal species such as bobcats, raccoons and skunks, as well as a number of migratory birds from Central and South America.

Highfields Lindbergh Estate

When famed aviator Charles Lindbergh first flew over spectacular Sourland Mountain, he was so captivated by its beauty that he decided to make it his home. In 1932, the Lindbergh family moved to a 23-room mansion on their 700-acre estate called *Highfields*. Today, the estate is operated by the State of New Jersey as a home for disadvantaged youth.

Sourland Mountain Preserve *(above and opposite)*

Sourland Mountain is covered with the largest
contiguous forest in Central New Jersey, nearly
ninety square miles in area. The pristine wooded
preserve, located in East Amwell Township, is an
excellent venue for bird watching, hiking, biking,
and rock climbing. Sourland Mountain Preserve
is a recreational haven in an undisturbed natural
setting.

Hillsborough Fair *(above and opposite)*

A festive Ferris wheel and a fun house with a German motif are just two of the many attractions at the annual Hillsborough Fireman's Fair. The fair, a week-long event in July, raises money to benefit local fire companies. Every year, fairgoers look forward to a growing variety of exciting rides, games, and delicious foods.

Hunterdon Museum of Art *(above)*

The Hunterdon Museum of Art is housed in an historic grist mill alongside a scenic waterfall in the quaint town of Hunterdon. A landmark regional art center, the museum exhibits works by established and emerging contemporary artists. The museum's permanent collection highlights prints by Mark DiSuvero, Philip Guston, Alex Katz, and Ad Reinhardt.

Hunterdon Historical Museum *(opposite)*

Across the river from the Hunterdon Museum of Art is the Hunterdon Historical Museum in Clinton. The landmarked Red Mill documents over 180 years of Hunterdon County history through exhibits of 40,000 artifacts. The 1810 mill once processed wool, grist, plaster, graphite, and talc while generating electricity on the banks of the Raritan River.

The Great Swamp Refuge

Just twenty-six miles from New York's Time Square is one of New Jersey's greatest natural treasures. The 7,600-acre Great Swamp Refuge in Basking Ridge covers a changing terrain of marsh, pond, meadow, wetland, and woodland. Paths meander through the natural environment, and educational centers at the swamp's entrances teach of the area's natural resources.

Pequest Fish Hatchery

One of the nation's foremost trout hatcheries, the Pequest Fish Hatchery, educates through interactive exhibits, displays, and video presentations. Located on 1,600 acres in Oxford, the hatchery annually produces over 600,000 brook, brown, and rainbow trout that stock hundreds of public fishing areas in the state.

Lakota Wolf Preserve

In the mountains of the Delaware Water Gap, the howling of wolves can be heard for the first time in over one-hundred years at the award-winning Lakota Wolf Preserve. Packs of Tundra, Timber, and Arctic wolves in a natural setting provide an educational resource to learn about pack behavior, social structure, eating habits, and how wolves play.

Delaware Water Gap National Recreation Area

Tiger lillies adorn the roadside in the Delaware
Water Gap where the Middle Delaware River is
nature's dividing line between Pennsylvania and
New Jersey. The national recreation area encom-
passes both sides of a forty-mile section of the
river and provides first-class opportunities for
outdoor enthusiasts.

Adventures in Nature

Adventures in kayaking, tubing, fishing, hiking and more await in the acclaimed Delaware Water Gap National Recreational Area that straddles New Jersey and Pennsylvania. In the distance, the Middle Delaware River curves to the right and flows between the highest peaks in the Gap, New Jersey's Mount Tammany on the left and Pennsylvania's Mount Minsi on the right.

Mountain Creek Resort *(opposite)*

Nestled in the panoramic Vernon Valley of Northern New Jersey, Mountain Creek Resort provides family entertainment all year round. Summer fun features a water park, mountain biking park, and an award-winning golf course. Winter transforms the facility into a first-class ski resort with dozens of trails, terrain parks, and the region's only Superpipe.

Acorn Hall *(above)*

A historic house museum, Acorn Hall is the headquarters for the Morris County Historical Society. County history is preserved through exhibits and collections of many priceless artifacts. Built in 1853, the stunning Victorian Italianate mansion has been home to many generations of the Crane Hone family, prominent Morristown residents.

Musical Machines and Living Dolls *(above)*

The diverse collections of the distinguished Morris Museum range from costumes and textiles to geology and anthropology. A new gallery showcases 150 pieces from the museum's Guinness collection of 700 mechanical musical instruments and figures. The extraordinary collection is one of the most significant of its kind in the world.

Morris Museum *(left)*

A rare, 1900 Luminaire fair organ is just one of many treasures in the Musical Machines & Living Dolls exhibit at the Morris Museum. Located in Morristown, the highly-acclaimed museum includes an extensive collection of nearly 49,000 objects. Hands-on art and science workshops, history discussions, and live performances are offered throughout the year.

New Jersey Children's Museum *(opposite)*

The Fire Truck exhibit at the New Jersey Children's Museum in Paramus provides children with an exciting opportunity to climb aboard and experience an authentic 1954 Ahrens Open Cab Fire Truck. The Children's Museum includes thirty different play and fun areas for all ages, such as a Ballet Studio and Dinosaur Cave.

Meadowlands Racetrack *(top)*

The distinctive bugle announces the start of the race at Meadowlands Racetrack, in Rutherford. Known for its thoroughbred and harness racing events, the racetrack hosts some of the sport's most prominent races that sometimes include elaborate opening ceremonies. The racetrack is located in the Meadowlands Sports Complex, along with Giants Stadium and Izod Arena.

A Mile of Excitement *(bottom)*

One of the country's top horse racing courses, Meadowlands Racetrack has two oval tracks with a surface of a limestone base and crushed stone dust cushion. The main track is a one-mile oval for harness and thoroughbred racing. The Turf Course is a 7/8th-mile oval for thoroughbreds only. Seating capacity is 40,000.

The Sport of the Common Man

In a display of grace, beauty, and skill, a powerful equine moves at a brisk trot while the driver holds the reins from his sulky. Thoroughbred racing has long been known as "the sport of kings," but harness racing with Standardbred horses gave racing to the common man, first between neighbors on back roads and, later, on world-class race tracks.

Meadowlands of Rutherford

The velvety-green Meadowlands consist of roughly 20,000 acres of wetlands, uplands, and development areas where the Hackensack and Passaic Rivers flow into Newark Bay. Once considered a wasteland, areas of the Meadowlands are now protected from encroachment and development. The fragile ecosystem supports diverse species of fish and waterfowl.

A Delicate Balance *(left and right)*

An abandoned silo in an overgrown field and a truck rumbling across a high bridge in the Meadowlands of northwestern New Jersey are fitting reminders of the delicate balance between man and nature. Nearly 8,000 acres of marshes in the Meadowlands are now protected by law. Naturalists have documented over 260 species of birds, of which 33 are declining, threatened, or endangered; 22 mammals, over 50 fish species, 51 bee varieties and 420 different plants.

William Taylor

After receiving an M.F.A. in the history of photography from Princeton University's Department of Art and Archaeology in 1982, William Taylor became founder and president of Taylor Photographics, Inc. For more than two decades, he has been acclaimed for his photography while working with world-renowned architects such as Michael Graves, Philip Johnson, Frank Gehry, Robert Venturi, and Robert Stern. Mr. Taylor's clientele includes several Fortune 500 companies as well as prominent advertising agencies in New York City. His photography has won hundreds of awards for builders, architects, and advertising agencies. His images often grace the pages of the *New York Times* and architectural journals.

A resident of both New York City and Princeton, New Jersey, Mr. Taylor has created an impressive collection of stock photography that includes images of his travels to India, Nepal, Patagonia, Peru, Central America, Iceland, Hawaii, and the American Southwest. Exhibits of his work include "New Jersey: Industrial Landscapes" and "In Focus: India and Nepal." His photographs may be found in numerous private collections. A selection of his work can be viewed at www.taylorphoto.com.

Mr. Taylor would like to acknowledge his ever-patient associate, James Godish, and his wife, Anna Chave, for their help with this publication and would like to dedicate the book to his wife and family.